This book belongs to:

_____

To my daughter, Ysabella.

−B. B.

To my son, Ken.

−Y. A.

Desert Animal Family Rhyme

Patrick the Piglet's Learning Adventures

by Belle Brown

Copyright © 2023 Belle Brown

ISBN: 9798358935686 (Paperback)

Further information may be requested by contacting the author directly at:
bellebrown.author@yahoo.com.

Desert Animal Family Rhyme

Patrick the Piglet's Learning Adventures

by Belle Brown

Illustrated by: Yoga Ariesta

Patrick was a curious piglet,
always eager to learn more.
He had heard about the desert
and wanted to explore.

He had to know how animals
could live somewhere so dry.
It must be very different
from his home in the pigsty.

The farmer had some business
in the desert. What good luck!
Patrick Piglet hitched a ride
on the back of the farm truck.

As soon as the truck arrived,
Patrick jumped down on the sand
and went to meet the animals
who lived on this dry land.

First, he saw a **BULL**–a male camel–
who met him with a laugh.
He said, "I'll introduce you
to my family–my **COW** and my **CALF**."

The camels had long eyelashes,
to protect their eyes from dust,
and big humps, so they could go days
without food if they must.

An ocotillo plant with spikes
had blossoms that were bright red.
A family of hummingbirds
drank from its flowers and were well fed.

The tiny birds—COCK, HEN, and CHICK—
weren't worried by the spines.
Patrick wouldn't go too close,
but the tiny birds were fine.

A male jackrabbit called a **JACK**
raced toward his burrow
where his **JILL** and **LEVERETS** were safe.
Patrick approached the furrow.
"What's the hurry?" Patrick asked.

"There are coyotes all around,"
the jackrabbit replied with a tremor.
"It's much safer underground."

Soon a **DOG**-a male coyote-appeared.
"Where did that jackrabbit go?
I need to catch food very soon
with my **BITCH** and **PUP**, you know."

But Patrick did not hear the dog.
His attention was elsewhere.
He pointed to a rock and said,
"Look, there's a lizard over there!"

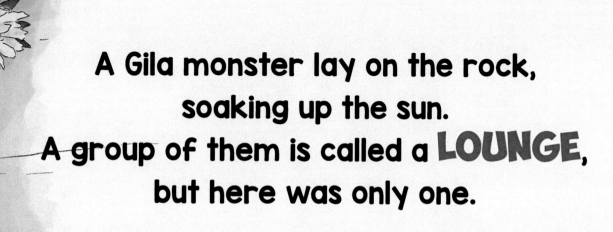

A Gila monster lay on the rock,
soaking up the sun.
A group of them is called a **LOUNGE**,
but here was only one.

Suddenly, something flashed by.
Patrick found it quite a stunner.
It snatched a scorpion with its beak.
It was the bird they call a roadrunner.

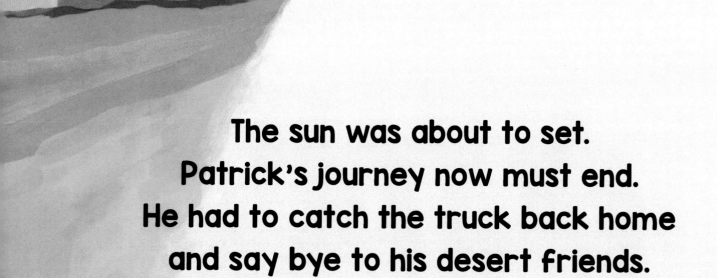

The sun was about to set.
Patrick's journey now must end.
He had to catch the truck back home
and say bye to his desert friends.

But just as he was leaving
and the sun lowered quite a bit,
a fennec fox family emerged,
the **DOG**, **VIXEN**, and **KIT**.

DOWN
1. a group of Gila monsters
2. a female coyote

ACROSS
3. a young camel
4. a female fox
5. a male hummingbird

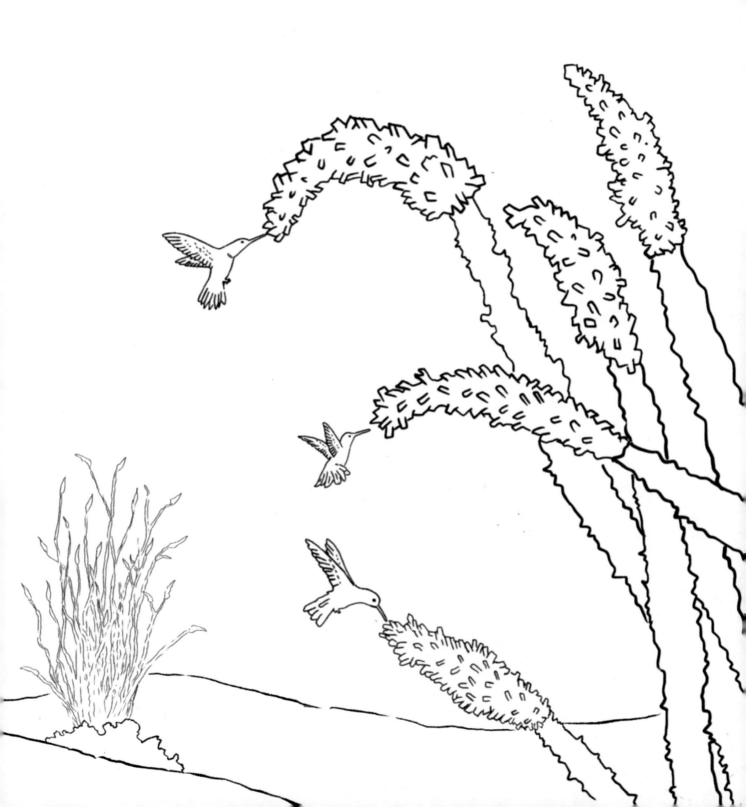

See You in Our Next Adventure!

Other books in the "Patrick the Piglet's Learning Adventures" series:

- Farm Animal Family Rhyme (Book 1)
- Patterns In Rhyme (Book 2)
- Shadows Follow, Echoes Rhyme (Book 3)

Like this book? Please consider leaving a review online. Your kindness and support are greatly appreciated!

Also written by Belle Brown

Nia the Narwhal Explores the Christmas Ocean

Yani the Unicorn and the Day Mommy Went to the Moon

Porcupine Hugs

Siv the Three-Toed Sloth

Dino Days with Terry T-Rex (COMING SOON!)

Please reach out:

belle brown.author@yahoo.com

https://www.instagram.com/bellebrown.author/

https://www.facebook.com/bellebrown.books